A CHILD'S DAY
IN A BRAZILIAN VILLAGE

To my daughter Victoria Maria, whom I was expecting at the time the pictures were taken and the text was written. Victoria allowed me to stay healthy and energetic, and inspired and encouraged me to climb up and down the hills around Cassiano's village.

Benchmark Books
Marshall Cavendish
99 White Plains Road
Tarrytown, New York 10591
Website:www.marshallcavendish.com

Library of Congress Cataloging-in-Publication Data

Campos, Maria de Fatima.
In a Brazilian village / by Maria de Fatima Campos
p. cm. — (A child's day)
Includes index.
ISBN 0-7614-1221-2
1. Maria da Fâ (Brazil)—Social life and customs—Juvenile literature. 2. Country
life—Brazil—Juvenile literature. [1. Brazil—Social life and customs.] I. Title. II. Series.

F2651.M346 C36 2001   981'.51—dc21   00-048595

Designed by Sophie Pelham

Printed in Singapore

1 3 5 7 9 8 6 4 2

AUTHOR ACKNOWLEDGMENTS
Special thanks to the following people and institutions for helping to make this book possible:
My husband, Richard Davis, and Mrs. Lilian Davis; Dr. Eugênio de Souza Cardoso, who dedicated lots of his time
to showing me around, and his mother, Dona Estela, who cooked delicious Mineiro food and looked after me; the Xavante children,
Sr. Antônio dos Santos, Zilda de Fatima Santos, the sugar mill of Sr. João da Luz, the sugar mill of Sr. José Vitor, Fazenda Pomária;
Sr. Domingos Tótora of the Oficina de Arte; Danilo, Vanessa, Luís Antônio, and Henrique; my friends Nensa, Fafá, Adriana, and
Maria Isabel Barbosa for checking the text; all the people of Maria da Fé, who gave their time and support, and
especially the Oliveira family, who made it possible for me to produce this book.

A CHILD'S DAY
IN A BRAZILIAN VILLAGE

Maria de Fatima Campos

BENCHMARK **B**OOKS

MARSHALL CAVENDISH
NEW YORK

AUTHOR'S NOTE

Probably the first thing that visitors to my country notice is just how mixed Brazilian culture is. It's all the different people who live here—Indian, African, and European—who help make Brazil such a unique and colorful part of the world.

Cassiano, "Cássio" to his family and friends, lives in a little village called Maria da Fé in the southeast of Brazil, in the state of Minas Gerais. Most people in the village know one another or are related in some way, and they all live together as one big family.

Maria da Fé is an especially good place to be a child. Cássio and his friends are as free as birds to play outside in the fresh mountain air and waterfalls, and to discover the world around them. When I visited and watched some of the traditional craftspeople at work, I felt as if I were stepping back in time. Brazilian life today is mostly very modern and busy, but in Cássio's village people lead much simpler, less hi-tech lives, and I think that makes it extra special.

BRAZIL

Minas Gerais

Cássio is six years old.

He lives with his parents, his older sister, Sara, and his younger brother, Luca. Cássio's mother, Júlia, is a teacher at the local adult education institute, and his father, Heraldo, is a bus driver. He takes students to the university in Itajubá, the nearby town.

Cássio's grandmother Angelina lives just a few minutes' walk away from Cássio's house. At six o'clock, when Cássio is waking up, his grandmother says morning prayers at her *oratório* (shrine). Like many people in Brazil, Cássio and his family are Catholics.

Angelina is holding a rosário (a string of rosary beads) in her hands. Each bead represents a single prayer.

When everyone is dressed and ready, the family sits down for breakfast. Cássio's father has bought some fresh *pão* (bread) from the bakery near the house. It is still hot from the oven and is delicious with *abóbora* (pumpkin) jam. They also have watermelon, cheese, cake, and *pão de queijo* (cheese bread). Cássio drinks orange juice and hot milky coffee.

COFFEE *is grown on plantations all over southern Brazil. There are many different ways to enjoy it—either with milk or cream, or as* cafezinho, *which is very strong, as* filter, *or cappucino coffee, or even as a refreshing cold drink over ice.*

On his way to school, Cássio stops to watch one of the women in the village making *queijo de minas* (cheese of the mines), the traditional cheese of Minas Gerais state.

MINAS GERAIS *means "General Mines," and takes its name from the mines in the area that used to be worked for gold, silver, and precious stones.*

Queijo de minas is very easy to make. Here the cheese is being molded into shape and squeezed until all the excess liquid is strained away.

Pão de queijo (cheese bread) is a local specialty and is made from strong *queijo de minas* and *polvilho*, a type of flour.

Next Cássio sees some horses making their way from the plantation to the sugar mill. The baskets on their backs are loaded with sugarcane.

SUGAR *(açúcar) production is an important industry in Brazil, and Brazilian sugar is sold all over the world. Senhor José makes his* açúcar *in the old-fashioned way, using traditional machinery and methods.*

The sugarcane arrives at the mill and Senhor José breaks it all up in order to extract the cane juice inside. He pours the juice into a big copper pan so that it can be heated.

As the juice gets hotter, its color changes from light green to gold, and it becomes a thick syrup called molasses. Senhor José pours the syrup into a trough and beats it with a wooden spoon until it cools.

At this local mill they specialize in *doce-de-leite* (milk candies). Milk is boiled with the sugar for a long time and then poured into wooden molds like these to cool and harden.

Cássio's class begins each day with a few minutes of prayer time. The class is silent so that the students can say their prayers to themselves in their own way.

It's very hot, so lessons are outside this morning. The children are learning about the Brazilian Indians, and what life was like for them before the Portuguese came to Brazil and made it their home too.

Cássio's mother has made him some chocolate cookies as a treat, and he shares them with his friends at *recreio* (recess). The snack will keep them going until *almoço* (lunch), which usually consists of beans, rice, vegetables, and meat.

Cássio doesn't stay inside for long, though. He wants as much time as possible to play soccer with his friends.

Later, the class visits a local crafts workshop. The artists here make bowls using a special mixture of cardboard and banana tree fiber.

The last lesson of the day is held in the school's *horta* (vegetable garden). Any vegetables that are ready are taken to the school kitchen so they can be cooked for lunch the next day.

Cássio and his friend Luís Antônio often push each other home from school in Cássio's *carrinho* (wheelbarrow).

They stop off at Senhor Élcio's candy store and buy some of their favorite candies, *doce-de-leite*.

When the children get too hot, they play in the little waterfall to cool off. Sometimes, during school holidays, Cássio and his family go to the seashore. Cássio loves paddling in the waves and making sandcastles.

Before going in, Cássio talks to his friend Senhor Antônio, who is making *balaios* (baskets). These *balaios* are used as containers in which horses carry sugarcane or bananas down from the mountain.

BALAIOS *Basketmaking is a traditional native craft. Indians use palm leaf, straw, or bamboo to make* balaios *in different shapes and sizes, and they carry all sorts of things in them—even their children.*

In this *galinheiro* (chicken coop), the farmer has filled some *balaios* with dry grass so that the chickens can lay their eggs in them. These chickens are called *caipira* (free range) because they don't have cages but are free to run around.

Cássio's mother has been to the market to buy food for dinner.
While she prepares the meal, Cássio goes upstairs to take a shower
and a nap.

Today is Cássio's father's birthday and the whole family has come to help celebrate. Cássio's mother has prepared beans, rice, salad, and beef. Uncle Paulo has brought *guaraná* for everyone to drink. Cássio's mother always cooks extra food in case someone arrives unexpectedly. In Brazil you don't need to ask beforehand—you can just drop in.

GUARANÁ is a very popular drink, and tastes best when ice-cold. It is made from the seed of the guaranazeiro tree, which grows only in the Amazon rain forest.

After dinner Cássio's great-grandmother reads him a story about the patron saint of Brazil—Nossa Senhora da Aparecida—while his parents watch a soap opera on television.

NOSSA SENHORA DA APARECIDA *is difficult to translate but means something like "Our Lady Who Appeared," because her statue once appeared in the nets of three Brazilian fishermen. The fishermen were amazed when they found her and believed that a miracle had taken place: They caught more fish that day than ever before!*

Even though it is bedtime, Cássio is still full of energy.

He sits up in bed and plays with his wooden truck until his mother comes to kiss him good night and turn off the light.

Dorme com Deus, Cássio (Sleep with God, Cássio).

MORE ABOUT BRAZIL

BRAZIL, THE PAST

Before people knew exactly what the world looked like, explorers used to go on voyages of discovery to conquer foreign lands. That's how Brazil came to be discovered in A.D. 1500 (about five hundred years ago), by an explorer from Portugal named Pedro Álvares Cabral. Brazil was part of the Portuguese Empire for the next three hundred years, and today's Brazilians are reminded of their history nearly all the time because the Brazilian national language is Portuguese.

When the first Portuguese settlers arrived in Brazil, they quickly discovered that it was a good place to grow sugarcane. But it wasn't until news spread that gold had been found in the mines in southeast Brazil that people realized just how much their new country had to offer them.

Apart from gold and silver, another important discovery was the rubber tree in the Amazon rain forest (imagine a world without tires or rubber bands!). These days, though, Brazil is probably most famous for its coffee. Coffee is grown in the south, where the climate, rich soil, and clean air provide the perfect conditions.

BRAZIL, THE LAND

Brazil is the fifth largest country in the world. It's so vast, it has four different time zones—which means that when it's nine o'clock in Cássio's village, it's only seven o'clock in Manaus, the capital of Amazonas state. Most of the country is in the part of the world known as the tropics, so it's hot all year round. It still rains, though, especially in the Amazon rain forest area in the north. People who live near the Amazon River have to build their houses on stilts because it rains so much between January and June that the land is completely flooded.

RELIGION IN BRAZIL

Many people in Brazil are Roman Catholic like Cássio and his family. The African religions Candomblé and Umbanda are also popular. Every New Year's Eve there's an *Umbanda* festival for Iemanjá, the goddess of the sea, and people celebrate at the coast and near rivers all over the country.

PEOPLE IN BRAZIL

Modern Brazilians are a mix of three different peoples: European, because of the Portuguese and other Europeans who settled in the country; African, because of the slaves who were brought from Africa into Brazil to work on the Europeans' sugarcane plantations; and Tropical Forest Indian, the people who were living in the region before anyone in Europe even knew that Brazil existed. It's all these influences that make Brazil such an interesting place to live. The Brazilian sunshine also helps to make people relaxed and friendly. Brazilians love to be by the sea, to listen to music, and to dance—especially the samba, which is danced at Carnival time, and the *capoeira*, a kind of fight dance. The Brazilian national dish, *feijoada* (a bubbling stew of pork and black beans), also dates back to slave times. The slaves used to make it from the pieces of pig that the slave owners didn't want to eat, such as the feet, ears, nose, and tail.

LANGUAGE IN BRAZIL

Most people in Brazil speak Portuguese, but the Brazilian Indian tribes also have their own languages. So far experts have counted more than a hundred different varieties, and there are lots of others they're still finding out about.

Brazil is the only Portuguese-speaking country on the continent of South America; everyone else speaks Spanish. With all their Spanish-speaking neighbors, it's not surprising that most Brazilians can understand a few Spanish words, although they might not be able to spell them. Some people speak Portunhol, a type of slang that combines Portuguese (**Portu**guês) and Spanish (Espa**nhol**). The Brazilian government would like more children to learn Spanish formally in school so that it will be easier for Brazil to do business with other countries in South America in the future.

The way a Brazilian person speaks also depends on what part of Brazil he or she comes from. It's a very big country, with lots of regional accents. This means that someone from Cássio's village in the southeast of Brazil would pronounce words quite differently from, say, someone from Salvador, a big city on the northeast coast.

SOME BRAZILIAN WORDS AND PHRASES

oi (oy)–hello

tchau (chow)–good-bye

está bom! (es-*sta* bom)–okay!

Como vai você? (kom-o vie vos-*say*)– How are you?

Qual é o seu nome? (qual *eh* o sell *nom*-ee)–What is your name?

THE PORTUGUESE WORDS IN THE BOOK

abóbora–pumpkin

açúcar–sugar, made from sugarcane, which
  is grown all over Brazil

almoço–lunch

balaio–basket

café–coffee

caipira–free range

Candomblé–a popular African religion

capoeira–a kind of fight dance

carrinho–toy car

doce-de-leite–milk candies

Dorme com Deus–"Sleep with God," a popular
  Brazilian way of saying "Sleep well"

feijoada–Brazil's national dish

galinheiro–chicken coop

guaraná–a soft drink made from guaraná seeds

horta–vegetable garden

Iemanjá–a goddess of the sea in one of the
  African religions

Manaus–the capital of Amazonas state in
  northern Brazil

mata burro–cattle barrier

Minas Gerais–a state in southeast Brazil

Nossa Senhora da Aparecida–the patron saint
  of Brazil

oratório–a shrine, or a special place for praying

pão–bread

pão de queijo–cheese bread, a specialty food
  of Minas Gerais

Pedro Álvares Cabral–the Portuguese explorer
  who discovered Brazil in A.D. 1500

polvilho–a type of flour used to make *pão de queijo*
  (cheese bread), made from the manioc plant

Portunhol–slang that combines **Português**
  (Portuguese) and *Espanhol* (Spanish)

queijo de minas–"cheese of the mines," a traditional
  white cheese

recreio–recess

rosário–a string of rosary beads, often used by
  Catholic people when they are praying

samba–the traditional dance of Brazilian Carnival

Umbanda–an African religion similar to Candomblé

FIND OUT MORE

Bailey, Donna and Anna Sproule. *Brazil: Where We Live.* Austin, Texas: Raintree Steck-Vaughn, 1990.

McKay, Susan. *Brazil.* Milwaukee: Gareth Stevens, 1997.

Serra, Mariana. *Brazil: Food and Festivals.* Austin, Texas: Raintree Steck-Vaughn, 2000.

INDEX